with an introduction by Edwin Mullins

The Art of Elisabeth Frink

Noyes Press

Noyes Building, Park Ridge, New Jersey 07656, USA

First U.S.Edition : 1973
Copyright © 1972 by Lund Humphries

Library of Congress Catalogue Card Number : 72–85246
ISBN : 0–8155–5012–X

Designed by Herbert Spencer

Printed in Great Britain

The publishers gratefully acknowledge the cooperation of
the Waddington Galleries, London

Contents

The main artery of Elisabeth Frink's work is the theme of the dominant male. The male is not always a man. He is frequently a beast, or a bird, or something between the two. Or a man with wings. Or a bird without wings. There are variations within the Frink bestiary, but they are all variations on that one theme – the dominant male. He is aggressive, mindless, physical and predatory.

More specifically, her work is a *female* view of maleness. The female viewpoint is very important. It sets her sculpture a little apart from the work of those rather older contemporaries with whom she was associated during the 1950's and early 1960's. This was the generation following Henry Moore and Barbara Hepworth that became internationally known as the first British School of sculpture. Other prominent members were Lynn Chadwick, Bernard Meadows, Kenneth Armitage, Reg Butler, Edouardo Paolozzi and Anthony Caro.

Elisabeth Frink was a good deal younger than they, and she was a woman. Her early work stylistically owed much to theirs : her images likewise, as well as the patched and ragged forms those images took. But the aggressiveness of her sculpture was subtly different. In nature and in viewpoint it differed because it was, so to speak, an observed aggressiveness : it was a female view of the male beast.

This female view was really one of fascination implying a certain detachment ; and as her work has progressed in the years since, this salutary note of detachment has grown louder and more distinct. She has become increasingly an observer, and this is a source of strength.

Elisabeth Frink was born in 1930, and studied art first at Guildford and then at Chelsea, where she was a pupil of Bernard Meadows. Henry Moore, she remembers, came to the school once or twice, and even absent his shadow loomed very large. It was while she was at Chelsea that he gained the main sculpture prize at the Venice Biennale in 1948. Meadows had been Moore's assistant, and his own work was still strongly under his influence.

Early visits to Paris brought her in touch with Giacometti, an awesome figure even then, and most of all with the work of Rodin at the Musée Rodin.

The nineteenth-century master's drawings and fragmentary pieces she admired most, the untamed side of him. Degas's bronzes she was drawn to as well, particularly the horses. And of course Germaine Richier, whose visceral distortions of form, and fascination for beasts, offer some of the principal antecedents of Elisabeth Frink's own sculpture, even though the surrealist content of Germaine Richier's work remained foreign to the English sculptor. While she never actually saw it, Picasso's *Man carrying a Sheep* was another key work in European sculpture at that period, as were the bronzes of Matisse.

While still a student Elisabeth Frink met Helen Lessore, director of the now-defunct Beaux-Arts Gallery and at that time the most enterprising dealer in contemporary art in London. Mrs Lessore exhibited her work in 1951. The selection included some primitive-looking figures in plaster, the fruit of profitable hours in ethnographical museums, and several ambitious religious subjects which revealed a concern for German art, Grünewald specially. There were also some powerful drawings of horses and riders, and a menacing-looking bird cast in bronze which the Tate Gallery soon bought (for £66). Both the predatory bird, and the equestrian theme, were to be leading motifs in her work over the next twenty years.

She also received some early commissions, a *Blind Man and his Dog* for Bethnal Green, cast in bronze (which didn't stop it being vandalised), and a *Wild Boar* in concrete for Harlow New Town. In 1953 the Arts Council purchased an example of her work. Meanwhile she taught regularly at Chelsea, and later at St Martin's School of Art. She held her first show at her present gallery, Waddington, in 1959.

The *Blind Man and his Dog* of 1956 seems to me her first distinctly personal statement. It is the first piece to shed the rhetoric which suffuses the early work. A quality of awkward serenity has entered this piece, a quality which recurs in all her best sculpture from this time onwards, even in pieces that are outwardly violent and full of menace. One of the appeals of Elisabeth Frink's work is the close and unexpected association of drama with repose, a repose that is almost bland.

Already in the *Blind Man and his Dog* her sculpture has acquired what was soon to become a characteristic de-boned look. Starched. All skin and muscle. Stiff-legged. The mind is made to ponder over what is inside. Certainly something soft : air perhaps, or water.

Such an effect is the direct result of a preferred way of working in very wet plaster, working fast, smoothing the surface, letting it dry, attacking it and breaking it up, doing it again until all forms become simplified, straightened out, details eliminated. Like other sculptors of the 50's she found carving too slow a process.

More typical of British sculpture at that period are a series of 'death's-throe' pieces representing dogs, cats and hens, twisted and corpse-like, lying on the ground or suspended from hooks : at the same time some equally 50's-looking dismembered torsoes.

Elisabeth Frink has always enjoyed drawing, and exploring in this medium possible future ideas for sculpture. Later, her lithographs and etchings come to fulfil a similar exploratory role, tackling themes not yet tackled in sculpture. The most striking drawings of the late-50's and 1960 dwell on two themes which are to create the mainstream of her sculpture for the next ten years : the predatory bird, and the spinning, falling figure.

The bird theme actually goes back earlier, at least to the bronze which the Tate bought in 1952 ; but now the theme becomes obsessive, as it grows freer and less naturalistic in form.

Beginning in 1961 there is a tendency to reduce the bird shape to a few powerful, menacing elements ; to elongate the legs and bill, shrink the body, so that the creature becomes all mobility and striking-power. The *Winged Beasts* of 1962 and 1963 carry this process further still. The 'Eagle' lectern commissioned for Coventry Cathedral in 1962 belongs to this family. By the mid-60's the idea is taken further again. The *Birds* of 1964, and the *Winged Figures* of the same year, are virtually all spindly legs and head. They are also less recognisably bird-like, far more abstract than their predecessors.

Her sculpture contains a mere handful of preoccupations : she evolves rather than invents. The other early, formative drawings were the studies of spinning, falling men which she did in 1960. These led to a series of *Spinning Men* in bronze, done in the same year, which continued the practice she had formed of making pieces without a plinth or stand of any kind ; but they were also the beginning of a long sequence of sculptures on the theme of man in flight : helmeted aviators and bird-men, metamorphic figures, launched horizontally with arms outstretched to defy gravity, and which recur in her work right up to 1966.

The early-1960's see the emergence of a number of Frink archetypes out of this rather scattered early material. The predatory bird and the free-flying aviator I have mentioned. Another is the single standing figure – *Sentinel* 1961, *Armoured Man* 1962, the various *Assassins* (actually double figures moulded into one) of 1963, *Judas* 1963, and the series of *Warriors* of 1963 and 1964. Each is at the same time threatening and threatened, a mythological figure as the titles suggest, owing a good deal to the contemporary work of Lynn Chadwick. Perhaps for that reason the series peters out after 1964, to return in a far more personal form during the late-1960's, no longer moulded by the prevailing idioms of the time.

Then there are the 'Heads'. These are in no sense busts : rather they are decapitated heads, bits of a body, rough in texture and chunky in form, made to lie or rest on a flat surface like the early torsoes and the *Spinning Men*. Beginning with *Fish Head* in 1961 a great number of these decapitated heads follow in the next few years. The heads are of animals for the most part, and are a refinement – if that is not too refined a word – of the morbid earlier studies of dead cats and hens. Like the rhetorical standing figures they peter out in the mid-1960's, perhaps for similar reasons ; but, again like the standing figures, they reappear in a new and more personal guise, in this case almost immediately in a transitional form – a group of *Soldiers' Heads* of 1963 and 1964 – and subsequently as those smoothed and puzzling Soldier-heads and Goggle-heads which have emerged intermittently since 1965.

The theme of The Aggressor, the threatening man-bird-beast, was one of the clichés of British sculpture during the 1950's and early-1960's. Much has been written about the character and pretensions of British sculpture during that era, and there is no need to add further comment except to note that without exception the sculptors concerned have either moved right away from the preoccupations of that period, or else they have faded into obscurity. In either case it was not a phase of British art which proved to have much stamina. It was an era, it now seems in retrospect, of false confidence : of rhetoric disguised as drama, of imprecise thinking masked by overstatement.

Elisabeth Frink's departure from the '50's style' has been less abrupt and less total than that of, say, Caro or Paolozzi, but she has moved away none the less, and into a no less personal idiom. She is the only outstanding sculptor of that generation to have moved back to naturalism rather than deeper into abstraction. The evolution of her single standing figures illustrates this progression well. We have seen how the early sculptures on this theme were rhetorical, mythological figures, full of menace, rough in handling, and owing much to the example of Lynn Chadwick ; and how this series petered out after 1964, to be resumed in the later-1960's in a more personal manner. But the evolution of ideas was not quite so clear-cut. As so often with Elisabeth Frink, there was a forerunner ; and that forerunner was a massive standing figure of a man, barrel-chested and with his left arm raised in an imprecise gesture above his head. The figure was over six feet tall, called *First Man*.

This was 1964, the year of the *Warrior* series of standing figures. But there was a marked difference between the two. The *Warriors* were typical, chunky, rhetorical figures of the 50's, in an idiom already something of a cliché. *First Man* is nothing of the sort. It is an archetypal Frink standing figure. It looks forward, not back.

What is new about *First Man* is evident if one compares him with the *Warriors.* Firstly, this is plainly a man, no longer some sort of armour-plated mythological creature. He is a nude man, what is more. The surface, which had once been rough and craggy, often in defiance of anatomy, is now almost smooth, thinned down in the legs and face, rounded out in the belly and chest. Most of all, no longer is he threatening, but monumental. He is a figure of awe, not of menace. He wears that placid dignity that is to become a characteristic of Elisabeth Frink's later work in bronze. Here is the prototype of the standing male figures who recur in the later-1960's, in the series of *Men with Goggles* of 1968, the lighter-weight *Shooting Man* of 1970, and in particular the smaller and larger versions of the horse-rider figures of 1969, 1970 and 1971, together with the shadowy pencil-and-wash drawings that are related to those *Horse and Rider* bronzes, as well as a number of the *Canterbury Tales* etchings of 1971–2.

Not surprisingly, the same evolution of style has overtaken the single heads. They, too, have emerged from a rather anonymous 'English' treatment of human and animal heads of the early-60's, into quasi-naturalistic studies of recognisable men – I say 'quasi-naturalistic' because the *Soldiers' Heads* and *Goggle Heads* that she has produced since 1964 are in no real sense portraits, though they certainly bear a quizzical likeness to her husband Ted Pool. These, too, are really archetypes. As with the standing figures, she has aimed at a monumental impersonality, in which any profound sense of portraiture is gradually smoothed away by her hand working over the wet plaster, a hand that at the same time builds up and exaggerates features like the chin and the forehead, adding seemingly incongruous details like a tassel at the back of the head, shining goggles over the eyes, or a strap fastening under the chin.

The predatory birds, so prominent an obsession in her sculpture of the mid-60's – and which made Elisabeth Frink her name – remain truer to their earlier selves than do the human images ; and maybe for that reason they have for the time being disappeared from her work. It is unlikely to be for long. The last series of these birds – several complementary series – were the *Birds, New Birds* and *Mirages* of 1965 to 1967, of which the *Mirages* represent the fullest and perhaps the ultimate development in the artist's search for the most simplified form to express a bird's gait and cruelty. The *Mirages* reduce the bird-form to a particularly evil-looking pair of wire-cutters.

Frink birds are earthbound. They stalk. They lunge. They menace. They even raise their wings. But they never fly. In the later examples they do not even have wings. And yet flight, forms in space, has been one of the sculptor's preoccupations since the early 50's. This is a puzzle. Why not combine two preoccupations ?

The answer, I think, is a key one in understanding the relation of Elisabeth Frink's work to naturalism, as well as the nature of those impulses and obsessions that guide it. If I gauge it right, representation of objects in nature has never been of much concern to her. I said at the beginning of this Introduction that the main artery of her work was a preoccupation with the theme of the dominant male, and that this male figure took many forms, most of them animals. What has mattered most of all in the sculptor's selection and treatment of imagery has been the way in which it has seemed to her to embody maleness. To her the maleness of a bird is embodied in its beak and its legs, and in the aggressive manner it employs these (note that long thin legs are also a feature of her sculptures of men). The flight of a bird is something altogether more graceful and quite different in its appeal. The maleness of a man, on the other hand, is of course more various ; but one of the strongest manifestations of it to the sculptor happens to be his endeavour to fly – to fly, that is, unaided, except with man-made wings. This is a personal obsession which has produced some of her most powerful sculpture.

The *Bird-Men* bronzes begin in 1962, and really evolve out of 'spinning' figures she started making in 1960. The first was a *Horizontal Bird-Man,* and there have been two very similar pieces since, in 1964 and 1966, in which a slender male figure is represented with arms and legs outstretched, launched in space. Far more numerous are the standing winged figures (on the launching-pad, so to speak), of which she made a good many examples in 1965 and 1966, the earlier ones called simply *Winged Figure,* the later ones *Homme Libellule* (Man Dragonfly). In both cases the human form is stretched upright, wings raised above his head.

The bronzes that come closest to naturalism are the pieces which, in appearance at least, are straightforward studies of animals. Three themes have been the subject of her sculptures : eagles, horses and wild boars, with a rather wider range of animals depicted in the *Aesop* lithographs of 1968 and to a lesser extent in the *Canterbury Tales* etchings of 1971 and 1972. Even here, though, the animals are representations of maleness first, and studies from nature second. (She never works directly from life, but from recollections.) In the process they have become in a sense mythological creatures, though the sculptor is emphatic that myth in the classical sense has no appeal to her whatever. Frink's creatures inhabit a world not so much of heroes as of day-to-day archetypal figures. It is a world in which there are neither hierarchies nor brains and in which distinctions between man and beast are vague.

The clearest representation of this man-beast relation in Elisabeth Frink's work so far has been the large *Horse and Rider* of 1969, of which two smaller versions were made in 1970 and 1971, and which exist besides in numerous studies in pencil and wash, as well as in one of the *Aesop* lithographs produced during the year preceding the large *Horse and Rider* group. This is her most literal interpretation of a man-beast theme that has been present in her work since *Blind Man and his Dog* of 1956, and has been more dramatically represented by the figures of bird-men and dragonfly-men where the two elements are fused into one. It is characteristic of the later work that dramatic renderings of the horse-and-rider theme appear only in the form of related drawings, while the sculptural group itself is all but stripped of drama, and presented in that stiff and slightly bland manner she previously adopted in the Goggle Heads and Soldier-Heads.

On one level the related drawings are simply observations of a man riding his horse; the horse alternately galloping, prancing, rearing up, lying down; the rider astride the horse, dismounted from it, asleep against it. But already in these variations one catches the fascination the artist has felt for this relationship between man and beast, which is not so much a relationship as a kind of unity. The most moving of these drawings are those in which the rider is represented not as the master of the horse at all but as the servant, supported and cradled by him. In one of the most gentle of them the rider is literally enclosed within the horse's limbs, as though he were physically a part of the horse, emerging from him.

Such is the instant recognisability of Elisabeth Frink's work that it is tempting to consider it immune from change. Indeed, the themes have not changed; but in treatment of those themes a considerable transformation has taken place. Her work used to be full of threat. Every piece, whether a bird poised to strike, or an armed warrior or a standing figure, adopted an attitude of aggression. That sense of threat has since evaporated. It still exists in choice of theme – *Wild Boar, Shooting Man* – but no longer in treatment. *Shooting Man* could be playing a clarinet without any change of mood. Even the wild boar, one of nature's fiercest animals as anyone knows who has heard them snorting and thundering in the forests, is represented as a creature whose natural aggression is submerged. It may be thought that with the disappearance of this aggression the fire has gone out of her work. It seems to me that it has gained in strength and personality by becoming more precise in form, less theatrical in content.

Sculpture is human experience made concrete. A sculptor may take images from life as an illustration, or as metaphor, or as symbol, adapting them to his purpose in the manner of a playwright treating a theme of historical fact. Only the bad sculptor handles images purely as an exercise in representation: then it is not human experience being made concrete, but mere faces and facts. Bad sculpture is the face of life fossilised.

Elisabeth Frink's sculpture is not particularly ambitious. The scope of her work finds natural boundaries in the images and experiences which engage her. Those boundaries tend to be narrow because these experiences are limited and consistent, the images repetitive. Her's is in the best sense traditional sculpture: she shows no signs of breaking faith with sculptural traditions established in the second half of the nineteenth century by Rodin and Degas, and extended during the present century by Matisse on the one hand, Giacometti and Richier on the other – positive and negative. The single heads and the *Horse and Rider* lie within the shadow of Matisse; whereas much of the earlier work, the standing figures above all, owes some debt to Giacometti and Richier – to the former the stylized elongations of forms and the surfaces built up and worked upon over and over until finally left in a state which suggests incompletion; to the latter the note of pessimism in the earlier pieces and the deliberate confusion of organic forms. Not that there has ever been anything in her work of Richier's morbid imagination, an imagination that made a romantic pursuit of the unfriendly aspects of nature in search of a metaphor for Fallen Man. There is none of that at all in the English sculptor; nothing whatever that is apocalyptic. Where Richier loved to dwell upon the skull beneath the skin, Frink has remained content with the skin.

The fondness for animals requires some historical comment. The Romantic painters in the early nineteenth century cast a new light upon animals. They were fascinated above all by the wildness of animals. Previously there had been no clear distinction in painting between wild animals and tame ones. But the Romantics loved savagery, and none more than Delacroix. His animals are far from the decorative creatures of the eighteenth-century painters, Oudry and Desportes. They have souls ; they know hunger, and hatred. Out of Delacroix's paintings of animals came a vein of sculpture in which animals were treated noticeably in Delacroix's manner, notably by Barye later in the century, and by Gaudier-Brzeska in the early part of the present century.

But there was another tradition of animal sculpture to emerge out of Romantic painting, and that was a naturalistic tradition, deriving more from Géricault than from Delacroix, and given its most eloquent expression in that marvellous series of horses modelled by Degas.

Then there were the 'Animaliers', as they were known. The 'Animaliers' were much lower down the scale. They emerged as a school during the latter part of the nineteenth century in response to an awakened interest in animals among the wealthy, particularly an interest in sporting animals. Heroic in concept, naturalistic in style, decorative in purpose, the work of the 'Animaliers' is a reflection of upper-class sporting interests during the Victorian era, and little more than that ; though there were a few talented sculptors among them, notably François Pompon, who worked for fifteen years in the studio of Rodin, and Rembrandt Bugatti, probably the best of them all, and brother of the great car designer.

These were the European traditions of animal sculpture that Elisabeth Frink inherited. Added to them was an important native tradition of animal painting, with Stubbs at the centre of it ; while, closer to her own time, there was the English Surrealist vein of animal painting, led by Sutherland and to a rather lesser extent Bacon, in which the principle of metamorphosis – derived from Picasso's work in the 30's – was firmly established, and distinctly in vogue during her student days.

Elisabeth Frink's own fascination for animals may be unknotted from this entanglement of traditions, but in personal terms it remains a more simple one. She was brought up in the country, rode horses from an early age,

and still does so ; living within reach of the Camargue in the South of France she finds ample opportunity to observe men on horseback, either rounding up the herds of black bulls that wander the scraggy water-meadows, or acting as decorative pieces of cowboy folklore. In either case what concerns her about the equestrian theme is the rider's control of his horse, the way horse and rider move as one : a physical contact, together with a kind of psychological understanding between two creatures. The wild boar theme is another that has emerged from her move to France, where in winter the boars emerge from the woods round her husband's vineyards in search of food, leaving their tracks in the mud.

Then there is the theme of Flight ; not, as I have pointed out, generally associated in Elisabeth Frink's sculpture with birds, but with men. Frink's Bird-Men find their earliest expression as spinning, falling figures ; only later do they become upright figures on the point of flight. The original impulse, in fact, was to make sculpture of a figure falling from space. The source here is dual. Since a child she has experienced dreams of herself falling, and the sensation remains a powerful one in her imagination. More specifically, during the late-50's she came across photographs of the French bird-man, Valentin, depicting him before he jumped (eventually he jumped to his death), helmeted and goggled, and decked out in his special flying-suit with voluminous wings.

This is the principal visual source of the various Bird-Men, though other ideas and obsessions play their part. There is always a multiplication of source-images in Elisabeth Frink's work. In 1966/7 a group of these Bird-Men suddenly fly under the title *Homme Libellule* (Dragonfly-Man). A second image, this time from nature, has merged with Valentin to shape the Bird-Man towards some ultimate archetypal creature. Actual dragonflies exist in clouds in the area of France where the sculptor lives. Their skill at being able to fly at speed and then to halt motionless in mid-air is an achievement beyond that of nearly all birds ; yet their life-span and evolutionary process is so rapid as to take place virtually before one's eyes. Elisabeth

Frink began to ponder on the possibility of man's life being subject to a similar evolutionary cycle, slowed down. Again, as with the image of Valentin, there is the suggestion of imminent death : the myth-figure which has emerged is fated. There is hope implied, but it is a futile hope. And it is this futility which excludes any real sense of tragedy, and which precludes any possible association with classical myth. It is significant that she does not call her bird-men 'Icarus'.

Frink birds, as we have seen, do not fly. They stalk. Like all her creatures they are an amalgam of what seem to her the essential characteristics of birds. Those essentials are to do with their predatory nature. The ultimate expression of that nature takes the form of the 'wire-cutter' figures which she calls 'Mirages', and here the evolution of a Frink archetype has been assisted by a strong optical impression. The title derives from the sight of birds seen from a distance across the marshes of the Camargue through heat-haze, which has the effect of appearing to flatten them against a wall of light, and of disembodying them.

Birds hunt to stay alive. So do animals. Restlessly. So does man when he has a chance, though his imagination offers him more sophisticated pursuits too, as well as a chance to earn his repose, and his pleasures. These are the kind of attitudes Elisabeth Frink's work has consistently projected. It brings me back to the theme of dominant male. To man the aggressor. The sense of threat, of menace, has departed from her work in recent years, but the themes have not changed. A sense of aggression is still implied in the images she chooses – man on horseback, wild boar, man with a gun, man with fierce-looking goggles.

The goggles are sinister. Sometimes they are merely part of an aviator's equipment. By the late-60's they have come to fulfil a different role : they are part of a disguise. First in the *Goggle Heads,* then in the standing figures with goggles, the element of threat is condensed into these disturbing, polished discs in front of the eyes, hiding the eyes, hiding whatever thoughts lie behind the eyes. The direct source is a crop of newspaper photographs which

appeared at this time of General Oufkir, a Moroccan who emerged into sinister prominence over the Ben Barka case which provoked a good deal more ghoulish interest from the French press than it did in ours in Britain.

Soldiers' helmets, aviators' gear, motor-cycle crash-helmets, Arab headdress, baseball players' protective clothing : Frink's helmet theme has been created out of an even more fragmentary jigsaw of images, pieced together in the artist's mind. Another Frink archetype ! Only the promiscuity of mass-media could have evolved so singular an obsession. Not surprisingly she talks with enthusiasm about Konrad Lorenz ('On Aggression') ; equally about a fascination for uniforms, which recall impressions of the war seen through the eyes of a young girl ; and about an awareness – though not more – of Henry Moore's own warrior figures and helmet heads of the early-50's. She points out that these were always classical images, not of our own time.

And she talks much about calm, about a dislike of theatre in art, about being 'anti-hero'. Her horse and rider are archetypal but anonymous : they move quietly through calm. Her goggled heads gaze out impassively, almost negatively. The tension-point of Elisabeth Frink's sculpture is precisely where a sense of peace and of threat coincide, wear the same disguise. Her work has shed the rhetoric of violence, to assume the more quizzical language of restraint. The temperature is low.

List of Illustrations

Sculpture

1
Warrior figure
early 1950's, plaster, 10/25·4
not cast

2
Warrior
early 1950's, plaster cast in bronze, life size
edition of 2

3
Tate Bird
1952, bronze, 18/45·7
unique

4
Dead Hen
1953, plaster, c.6/15·2
not cast

5
Dead Hen
another view of 4

6
Eleanor Billingham-Smith
1955, plaster, life size
not cast

7
First Holland Park sculpture
c.1955, plaster, detail from 6′ seated figure
destroyed

8
Falling Man
c.1956, plaster, L 14/35·6
not cast

9
Falling Man
another view of 8

10
Dead Cat
c.1956, plaster, c.30/76·2
not cast

11
Dead Cat
another view of 10

12
Blind Beggar and Dog
1957, bronze, 14/35·6
edition of 4

13
Bird
1957, bronze, c.20/50·8
edition of 6

14
Dead Hen
1957, bronze, 6½/16·5
edition of 6

15
Cock
1957, bronze, 25/63·5
edition of 6

16
Head
1958, plaster, 15½/39·4
edition of 4

17
Head
1959, bronze, 9/22·9
edition of 6

18
Bird
1959, bronze, 17½/44·4
edition of 6

19
Bird
1959, bronze, 15¾/40
edition of 6

20
Torso
1950–9, bronze, L 60/182·9
edition of 3

21
Winged Figure
1960, bronze, 36/91·4
edition of 4

22
Spinning Man II
1960, bronze, L 19/48·2
edition of 3

23
Fallen Bird Man
1961, bronze, L 72/182·9
edition of 3

24
Spinning Man
1960, bronze, 18/45·7
edition of 6

25
Cat
1960, bronze, 6/15·2
edition of 3

26
Dormant Head
1961, bronze, 7½/19·1
edition of 6

27
Fish Head
1961, bronze, 9/22·9
edition of 6

28
Little Bird
1961, bronze, 10/25·4
edition of 10

29
Small Bird
1961, bronze, 12/30·5
edition of 9

30
Sentinel
1961, bronze, 51/129·5
edition of 4

All dimensions are given in inches/centimetres and refer to height unless marked L

31
Sentinel
another view of 30

32
Small Winged Figure
1961, bronze, 17½/44·4
edition of 10

33
Falling Man
1961, bronze, 27½/69·9
edition of 6

34
Sentinel
1962, bronze, 34/86·4
edition of 6

35
Armoured Man
1962, bronze, 34/86·4
edition of 6

36
Eagle (lectern for Coventry Cathedral)
1962, bronze, 18/45·7
edition of 6

37
Horizontal Bird Man II
1962, bronze, L 13/33
edition of 8

38
Birdman
1962, bronze, 31½/80
edition of 6

39
Birdman
another view of 38

40
Winged Beast II
1962, bronze, 14½/36·8
edition of 8

41
Winged Beast II
another view of 40

42
Plant Head
1963, bronze, L 29/73·7
edition of 6

43
Horsehead
1963, bronze, L 75/190·5
edition of 6

44
Judas
1963, bronze, 75/190·5
edition of 3

45
Warrior
1963, bronze, 24¼/61·6
edition of 6

46
Dead King
1963, bronze, L 63/160
edition of 3

47
Carapace II
1963, bronze, L 24/60·9
edition of 6

48
Carapace II
another view of 47

49
Assassins I
1963, bronze, 22/55·9
edition of 7

50
Assassins II
1963, bronze, 20½/52·1
edition of 8

51
Small Eagle
1963, bronze, 9¼/23·5
edition of 8

52
Small Soldier's Head
1964, bronze, 6¼/16
edition of 7

53
Soldier
1963, bronze, 14/35·6
edition of 6

54
Soldier's Head
1964, bronze, 18/45·7
edition of 6

55
Warrior II
1964, bronze, 19/48·2
edition of 8

56
Bird
1964, bronze, 20/50·8
edition of 7

57
Bird
another view of 56

58
Warrior II
1964, bronze, 19/48·2
edition of 8

59
Small Bird II
1964, bronze, 14/35·6
edition of 7

60
Horizontal Birdman III
1964, bronze, L 13½/34·3
edition of 8

61
Plant Head
1964, bronze, 29/73·7
edition of 6

62
First Man
1964, bronze, 76/193
edition of 3

63
First Man
another view of 62

64
Study for Standard
1965, bronze, 10⅞/27·6
unique

65
Study for Standards I-VI
1965, bronze I 20¾/52·7, II 20/50·8,
III 20/50·8, IV 19¾/50·2, V 17½/44·4,
VI 16/40·6
all in editions of 8

66
Standard
1965, bronze, 74¼/188·7
edition of 3

67
Standard
1965, bronze, 74¼/188·7
edition of 3

68
New Bird II
1965, bronze, 15¼/38·7
edition of 6

69
Winged Figure III
1965, bronze, 17½/44·4
edition of 7

70
Soldier's Head I
1965, bronze, 14¼/36·2
edition of 6

71
Soldier's Head III
1965, bronze, 14/35·5
edition of 6

72
Soldier's Head IV
1965, bronze, 14/35·5
edition of 6

73
Soldier's Head IV
another view of 72

74
New Bird I
1965, bronze, 21½/54·6
edition of 6

75
Birds
1965, bronze, 8½/21·6, 10/25·4, 8½/21·6
all unique

76
Homme Libellule I
1965, bronze, 16½/41·9
edition of 6

77
Homme Libellule II
1965, bronze, 15/38·1
edition of 6

78
Wild Boar
1966, bronze, 6¼/15·9
edition of 7

79
Homme Libellule III
1966, bronze, 18/45·7
edition of 7

80
Homme Libellule III
another view of 79

81
Homme Libellule IV
1966, bronze, 19/48·2
edition of 7

82
Big Bird
1966–7, bronze, c.20/50·8
edition of 6

83
Bird
1966, bronze, 13⅞/35·2
edition of 6

84
Bird
1966, bronze, 17/43·2
edition of 7

85
Bird with Wing
1966, bronze, 20/50·8
edition of 6

86
Flying Figure
1966, bronze, L 13/33
edition of 7

87
Wild Boar
1967, bronze, 6¼/15·9
edition of 7

88
Wild Boar
1967, bronze c.30/76·2
edition of 4

89
Bronze Plaque
1967, bronze, 8¾/22·2
edition of 8

90
Mirage Bird
1967, aluminium, 84/213·4
edition of 3

91
Mirage II
1967, bronze, c.36/91·4
edition of 5

92
Mirage I
1967, bronze, 35¾/90·8
edition of 5

93
Mirage
1967, bronze, 33/83·8
edition of 6

94
Goggle Head (teeth)
1967, bronze, 20/50·8
edition of 6

95
Goggle Head (teeth)
another view of 94

96
Head with Goggles
1967, bronze, 20/50·8
edition of 6

97
Head
1967, bronze, 21¾/55·2
edition of 6

98
Man with Goggles
1968, bronze 19½/49·5
edition of 7

99
Small Walking Goggle Man
1968, bronze, 18/45·7
edition of 7

100
Small Walking Goggle Man
1968, bronze, 18/45·7
edition of 7

101
Maquette for Crucifix, Liverpool
1968, bronze, 11½/29·2
unique

102
Boar
1969, bronze, 7/17·8
edition of 7

103
Boar
1969, bronze, 44/111·8
edition of 3

104
Boar
another view of 103

105
Horse and Rider
1969, plaster for bronze 90½/229·8
edition of 3

106
Horse and Rider
another view of 105

107
Horse and Rider
another view of 105

108
Horse and Rider
another view of 105

109
Mirage I
1969, aluminium, 108/274·3
unique

110
Head with Goggles (teeth)
1969, bronze, 25½/64·7
edition of 6

111
Head with Goggles (no teeth)
1969, bronze, 25½/64·7
edition of 6

112
Man with Goggles
1969, bronze, 44/111·7
edition of 6

113
Shooting Man
1970, bronze, 21/53·3
edition of 7

114
Man on a Horse
1970, bronze, 19¾/50·2
edition of 7

115
Small Boar
1971, plaster for bronze, 4½/11·4

116
Small Boar
another view of 115

117
Lying Down Horse
1971, bronze, 13/33
edition of 6

118
Larger Rolling Over Horse
1972, bronze, 15/38·1
edition of 6

119
Sleeping Horse
1972, bronze, life size
edition of 4

Lithographs

120
Owl
1967, 30½×23/77·5×58·4
edition of 25

121
Wild Dog
1967, 31¼×23/79·4×58·4
edition of 25

122
Horse
1967, 30½×23¼/77·5×59·1
edition of 25

123
Hare
1967, 23¼×30½/59·1×77·5
edition of 70

124
Goat
1967, 30½×23½/77·5×59·7
edition of 25

125
Lioness
1967, 30½×23½/77·5×59·7
edition of 25

126
Boar
1970, 21¼×25¾/54×65·4
edition of 70

127
Bear
1970, 21¼×25¾/54×65·4
edition of 70

128
Man and Horse I
1971, 23½×31½/59·7×80
edition of 70

129
Man and Horse II
1971, 23½×31½/59·7×80
edition of 70

130
Man and Horse IV
1971, 23½×31½/59·7×80
edition of 70

131
Man and Horse V
1971, 23½×31½/59·7×80
edition of 70

132
Man and Horse VI
1971, 23½×31½/59·7×80
edition of 70

133
Horse and Rider IV
1970, 23×30½/58·4×77·5
edition of 70

134
Boar
1967, 31¼×23¼/79·4×59·1
edition of 25

Etchings

The Canterbury Tales
1972, 31½×22¾/80×57·8
edition of 50

135
The Franklin's Tale

136
The Summoner's Tale

137
The Miller's Tale I

138
The Miller's Tale II

139
The Clerk's Tale

140
The Prologue

141
The Nun's Priest's Tale

142
Sir Topaz

143
The Merchant's Tale

144
The Reeve's Tale

145
The Second Nun's Tale

146
The Knight's Tale

147
The Pardoner's Tale

148
The Prioress's Tale

149
The Shipman's Tale

Biographical notes and list of exhibitions

1930	Born at Thurlow in Suffolk
1946	Entered Guildford Art School
	Chelsea Art School
	Taught Chelsea Art School for 10 years
	Taught St Martin's College of Art
	Visiting Instructor Royal College of Art
1957	Commissioned by Harlow New Town
	Commissioned for new housing scheme Bethnal Green
1958	Joined the Waddington Galleries
1960	Commissioned for façade of Carlton Tower

One-man exhibitions

1955	St George's Gallery, London
1959	Waddington Galleries, London
	Bertha Schaefer Gallery, New York
1961	Waddington Galleries, London
	Felix Landau Gallery, Los Angeles
	Bertha Schaefer Gallery, New York
1963	Waddington Galleries, London : sculpture
1967	Waddington Galleries, London : recent sculpture
1968	Waddington Galleries, London : drawings from Aesop's Fables
1969	Waddington Galleries, London : drawings
	Waddington Galleries, London : drawings and sculpture
1970	Curwen Gallery, London
1971	Waddington Galleries, London : lithographs, etchings and sculpture
1972	Waddington Galleries, London

Group exhibitions

1951	London Group, Beaux Arts Gallery, London
1954	Open Air Exhibition, Holland Park, London
1955–6	Touring exhibitions in Sweden and Germany
1956	Aldeburgh Festival, Suffolk
1957	John Moore's Exhibition, Liverpool
	Open Air Exhibition, Holland Park, London
1959	Antwerp, Biennale at Middelheim Park
	John Moore's Exhibition, Liverpool
1960	Open Air Exhibition, Battersea Park, London
1970	Waddington Fine Arts, Montreal
1971	Summer Exhibition, Royal Academy, London
	Mixed Exhibition, The Park Square Gallery, Leeds
	Mixed Exhibition, Balcombe Galleries, Sussex
1972	204th Summer Exhibition, Royal Academy, London

Bibliography

Bernstein, Marcelle:
'Frink' in *Observer Magazine,* 30 November 1969, p.52f.

Burr, James:
'The Monster in Man' in *Apollo,* November 1970.

Fisher, Chris:
'Spine-chilling Heads: Elisabeth Frink' in *Eastern Daily Press,* 28 April 1972.

Gray, Robert:
'Frink, Bratby, Barnes, Jackson, East Kent and Folkestone Arts Centre, 1968

Kirkman, Terry and Judy Heviz:
'Arctic Determines Eskimo Sculpture' in *The Montreal Star,* 25 November 1970.

Raphael, Diana:
'Gallery Reviews: Elisabeth Frink' in *Arts Review,* 18 January 1969, p.18.

Reid, Sir Norman:
'Art within Reach' in *Observer Magazine,* 11 October 1970.

Roscini:
'Dual Surprise at Balcombe Exhibition', in *Sutton Herald, Epsom and Ewell Herald,* 9 December 1971.

Stockwood, Jane:
'Seven Figures in the Artscape' in *Harper's Queen,* March 1971, p.82.

Stockwood, Jane:
'Queen's Counsel' in *Harper's Queen,* August 1971.

Sculpture

1 **Warrior figure** plaster not cast 10/25·4 early 1950's
2 (right) **Warrior** plaster cast in bronze (life size) edition of 2 early 1950's

3 **Tate Bird** bronze 18/45·7 unique 1952

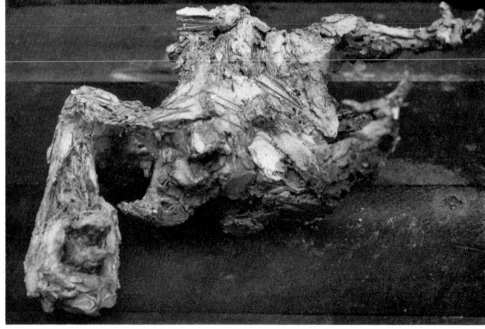

4 **Dead Hen** plaster not cast c.6/15·2 1953
5 another view of 4

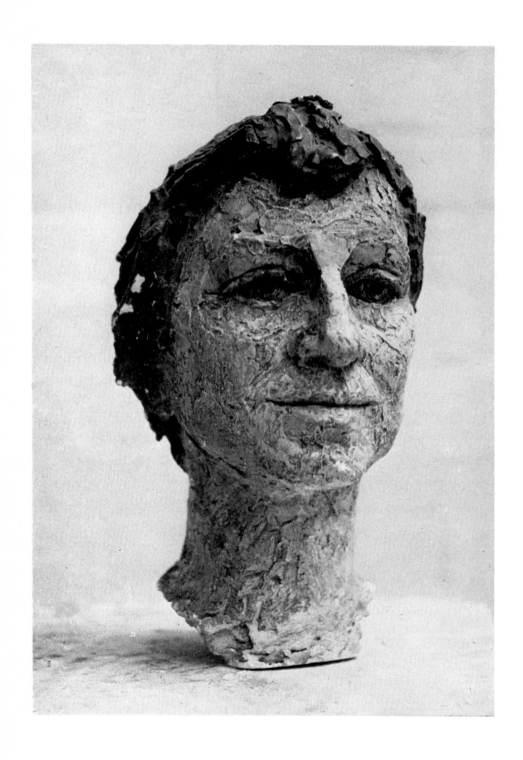

6 (above) **Eleanor Billingham-Smith** plaster not cast (life size) 1955

7 (right) **First Holland Park sculpture** plaster detail from 6' seated figure c.1955 destroyed

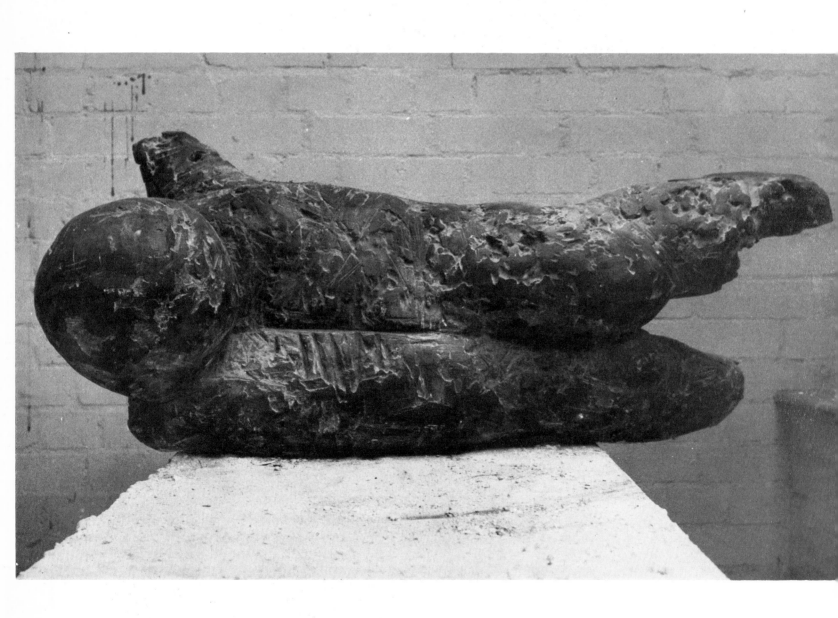

8 **Falling Man** plaster L14/35·6 not cast c.1956

other view of 8

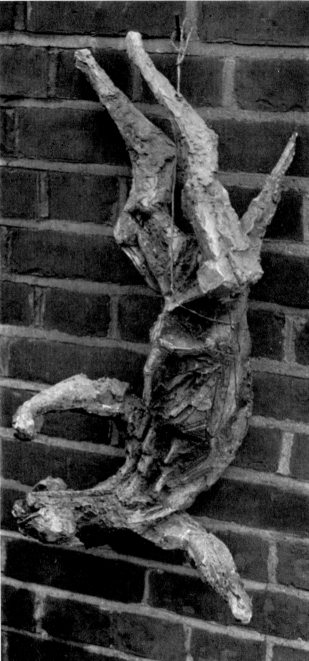

10 **Dead Cat** plaster c.30/76·2 not cast c.1956
11 another view of 10
12 (opposite) **Blind Beggar and Dog** bronze 14/35·6 edition of 4 1957

13 **Bird** bronze c.20/50·8 edition of 6 1957

ead Hen bronze 6½/16·5 edition of 6 1957

15 **Cock** bronze 25/63·5 edition of 6 1957

16 **Head** plaster 15½/39·4 edition of 4 1958

Head bronze 9/22·9 edition of 6 1959

18 **Bird** bronze 17½/44·4 edition of 6 1959

Bird bronze 15¾/40 edition of 6 1959

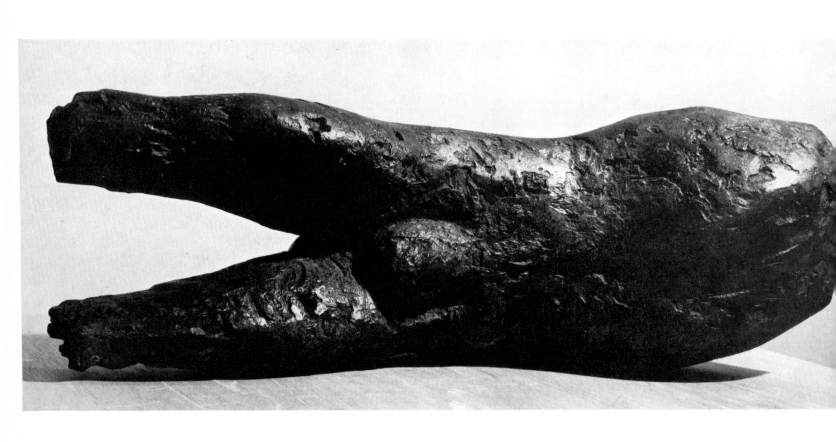

20 **Torso** bronze L 60/182·9 edition of 3 1950—9

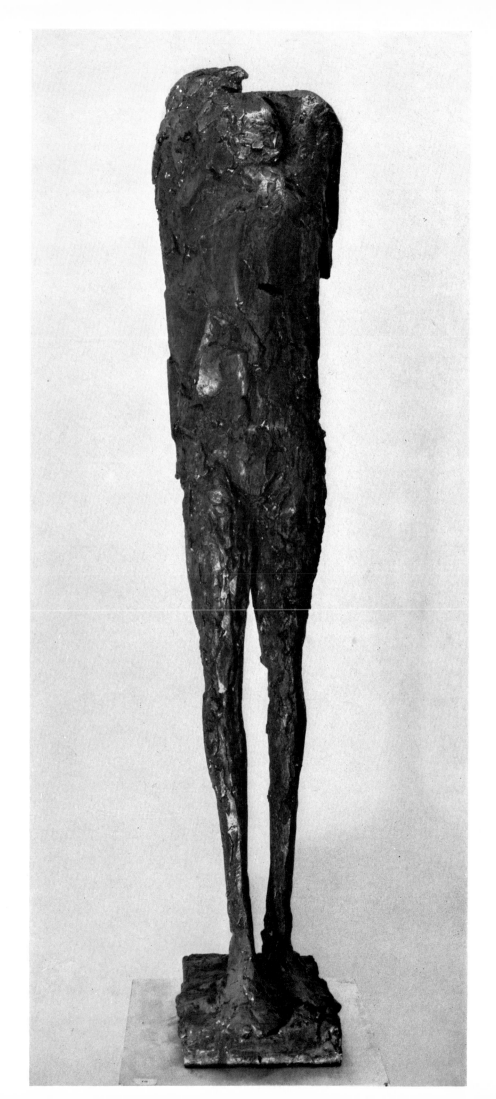

21 **Winged Figure** bronze 36/91·4
edition of 4 1960

22 **Spinning Man II** bronze L 19/48·2 edition of 3 1960

Fallen Bird Man bronze L 72/182·9 edition of 3 1961

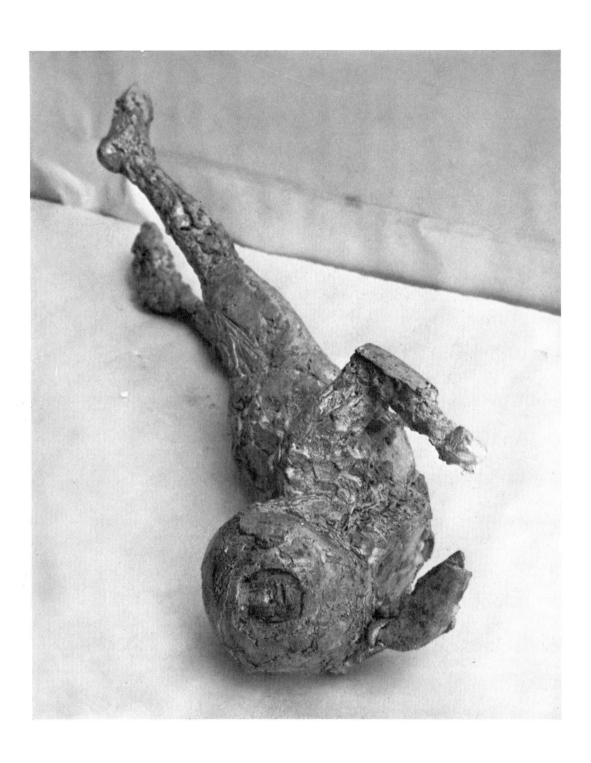

24 **Spinning Man** bronze 18/45·7 edition of 6 1960

Cat bronze 6/15·2 edition of 3 1960

26 **Dormant Head** bronze 7½/19·1 edition of 6 1961

Fish Head bronze 9/22·9 edition of 6 1961

28 (above) **Little Bird** bronze 10/25·4 edition of 10 1961
29 (opposite) **Small Bird** bronze 12/30·5 edition of 9 1961

30 Sentinel
bronze 51/129·5 edition of 4 1961

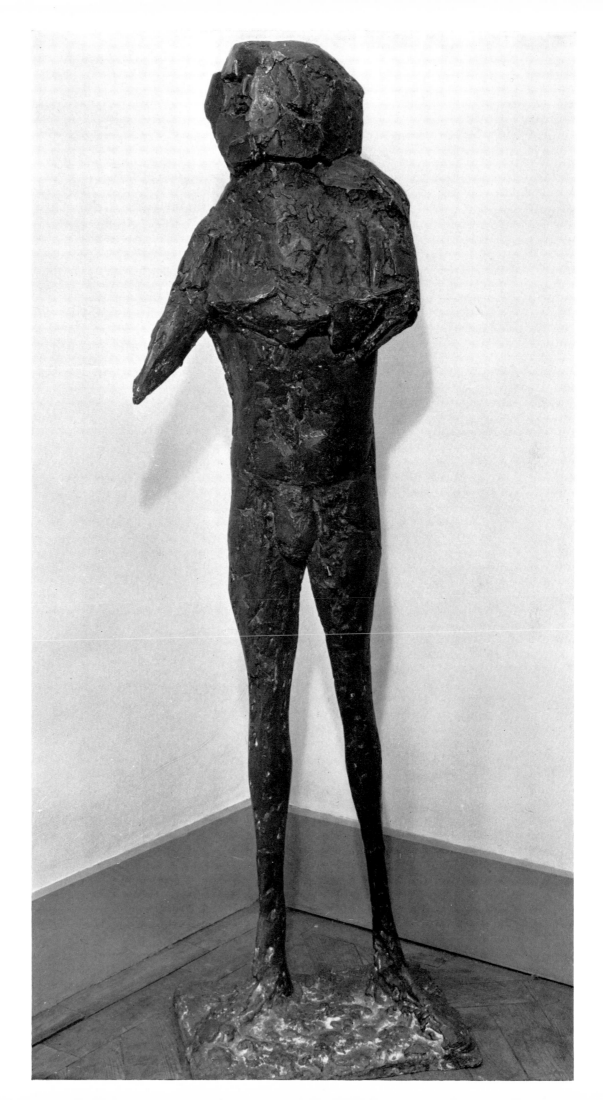

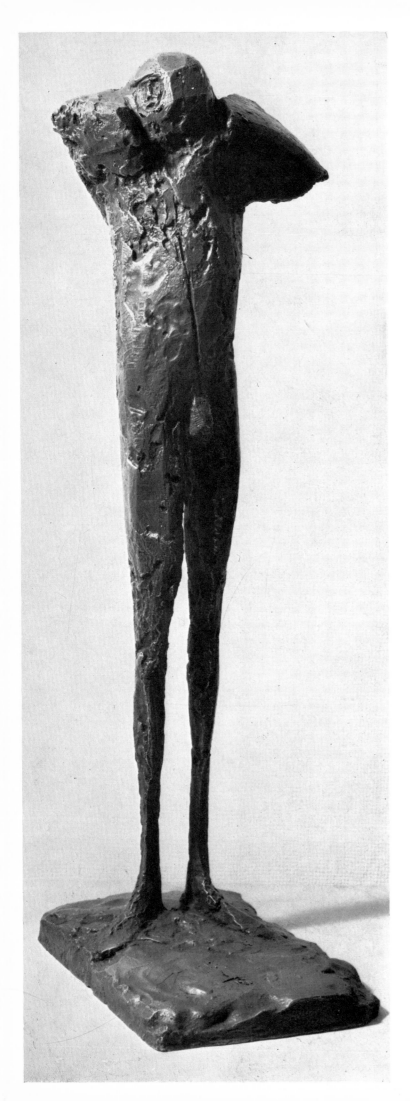

32 (left) **Small Winged Figure** bronze 17½/44·4 edition of 10 1961
33 (right) **Falling Man** bronze 27½/69·9 edition of 6 1961

34 Sentinel
bronze 34/86·4 edition of 6 1962

Armoured Man

onze 34/86·4 edition of 6 1962

36 **Eagle** (lectern for Coventry Cathedral) bronze 18/45·7 edition of 6 1962

Horizontal Bird Man II bronze L 13/33 edition of 8 1962

38 **Birdman** bronze 31½/80 edition of 6 1962

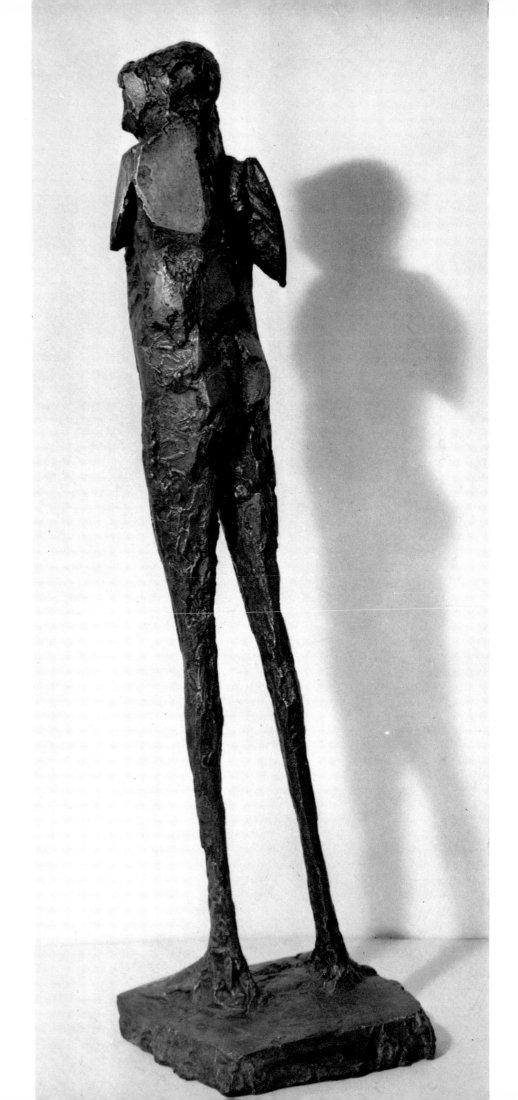

another view of 38

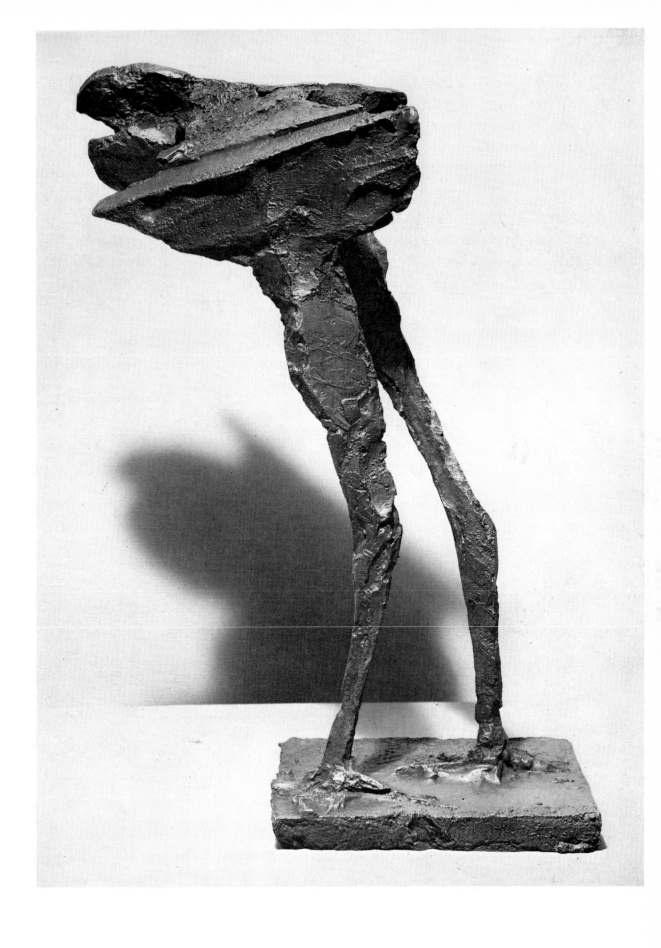

40 (opposite) **Winged Beast II** bronze 14½/36·8 edition of 8 1962

41 (above) another view of 40

42 **Plant Head** bronze L 29/73·7 edition of 6 1963

Horsehead bronze L 75/190·5 edition of 6 1963

(left)
Ias
nze 75/190·5
:ion of 3
3

(right)
rrior
nze 24¼/61·6
tion of 6
3

Dead King bronze L63/160 edition of 3 1963

47 **Carapace II** bronze L 24/60·9 edition of 6 1963

another view of 47

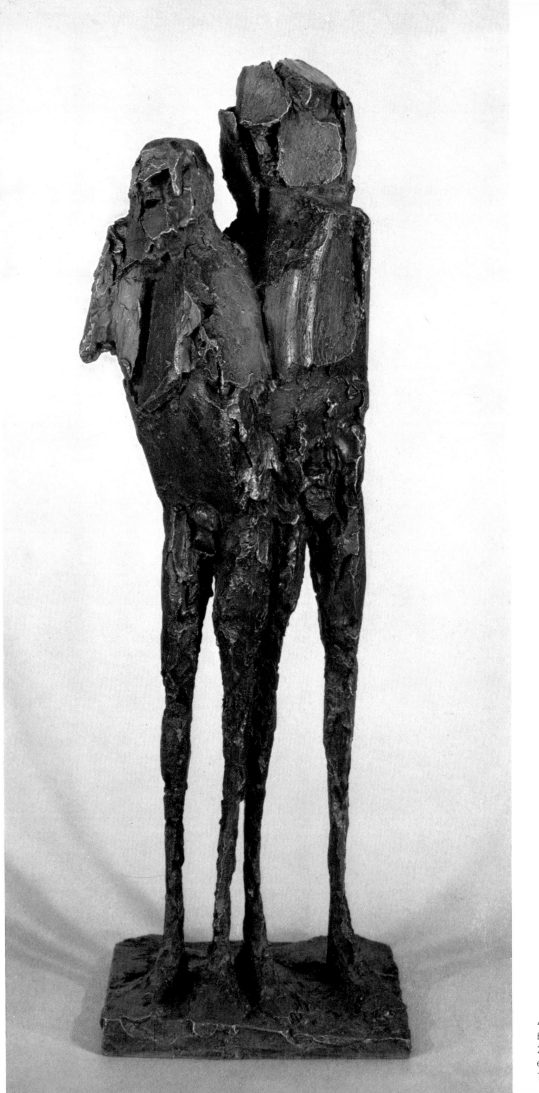

49 **Assassins I**
bronze
22/55·9
edition of 7
1963

Assassins II
onze
)½/52·1
lition of 8
63

Small Eagle bronze 9¼/23·5 edition of 8 1963

52 (above) **Small Soldier's Head** bronze 6¼/16 edition of 7 1964

53 (opposite) **Soldier** bronze 14/35·6 edition of 6 1963

54 (above) **Soldier's Head** bronze 18/45·7 edition of 6 1964
55 (opposite) **Warrior II** bronze 19/48·2 edition of 8 1964

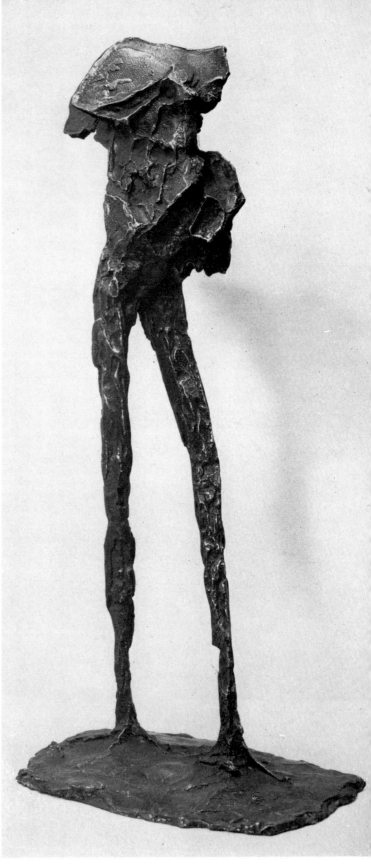

56 **Bird** bronze 20/50·8 edition of 7 1964
57 another view of 56

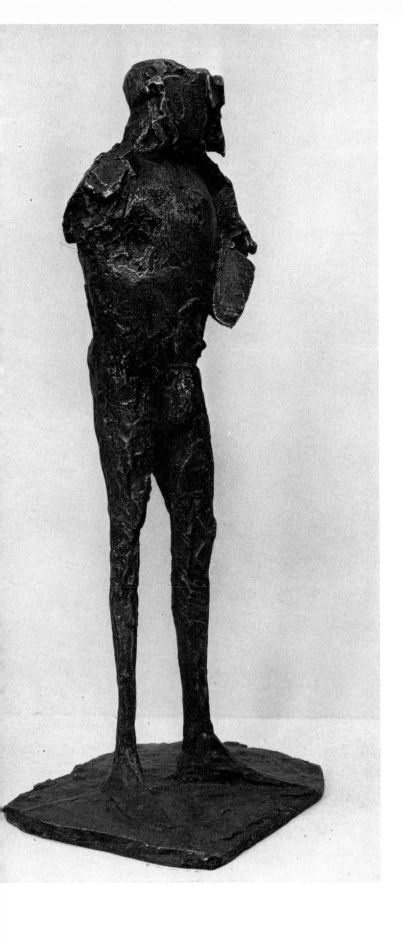

8 **Warrior II** bronze 19/48·2 edition of 8 1964

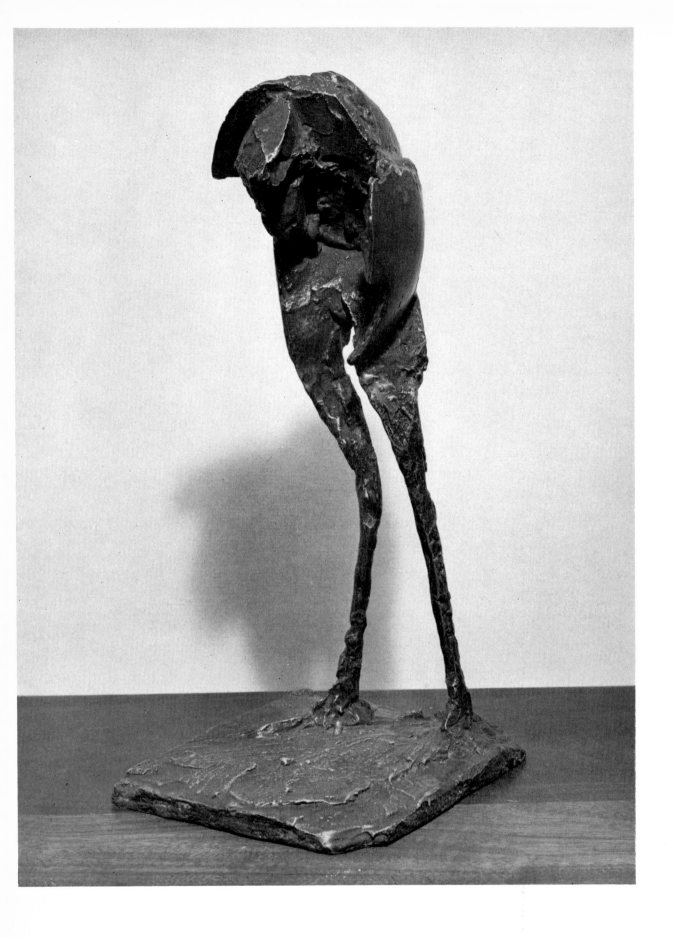

59 **Small Bird II** bronze 14/35·6 edition of 7 1964

Horizontal Birdman III bronze L 13½/34·3 edition of 8 1964

61 **Plant Head** bronze 29/73·7 edition of 6 1964

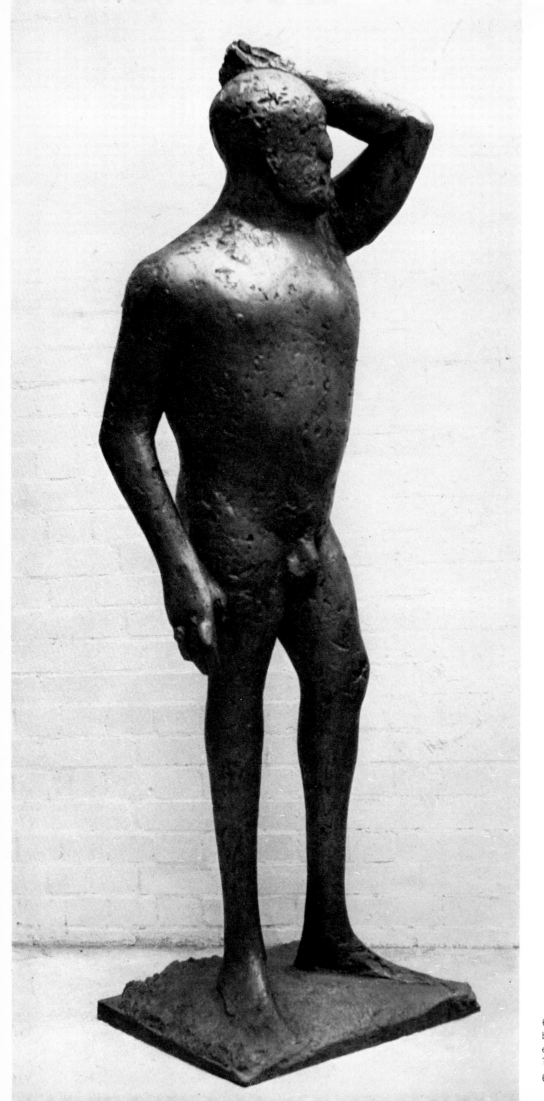

62 First Man
bronze 76/193
edition of 3
1964

63 (opposite) another view of 62

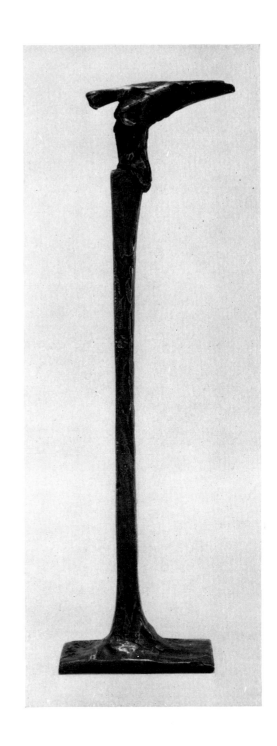

64 Study for Standard
bronze 10⅞/27·6
unique 1965

Study for Standards I–VI bronze I 20¾/52·7, II 20/50·8, III 20/50·8, IV 19¾/50·2, V 17½/44·4, VI 16/40·6 all in editions of 8 1965

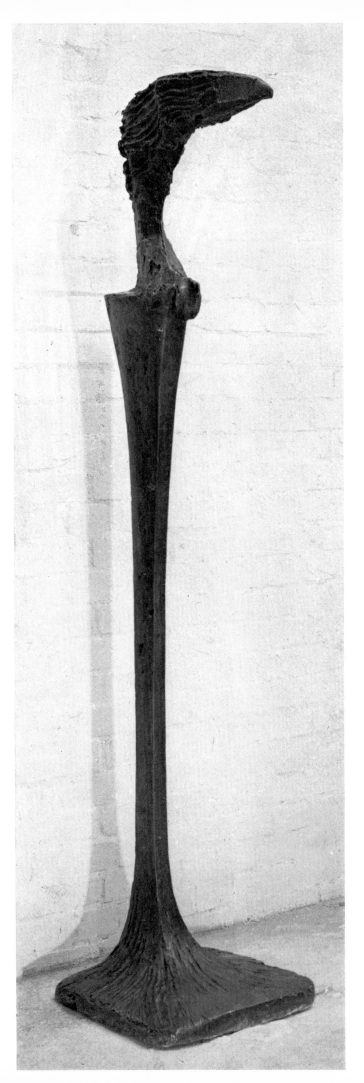

66 **Standard** bronze 74¼/188·7 edition of 3 1965
67 (opposite) **Standard** bronze 74¼/188·7 edition of 3 1965

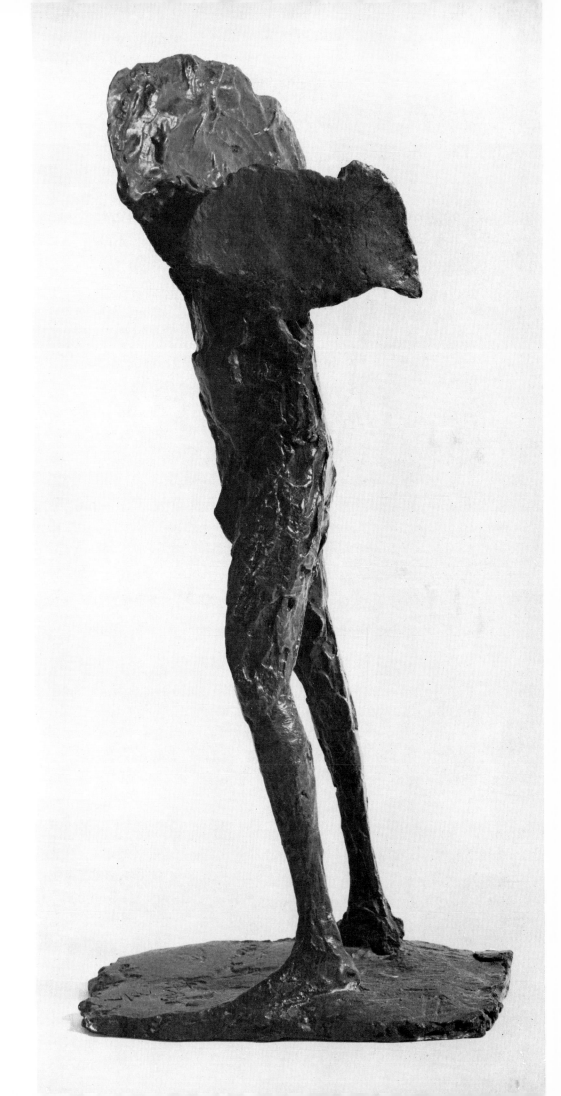

7 (left) **New Bird II**
onze 15¼/38·7
ition of 6 1965

8 **Winged Figure III**
onze 17½/44·4
ition of 7 1965

70 **Soldier's Head I** bronze 14¼/36·2 edition of 6 1965

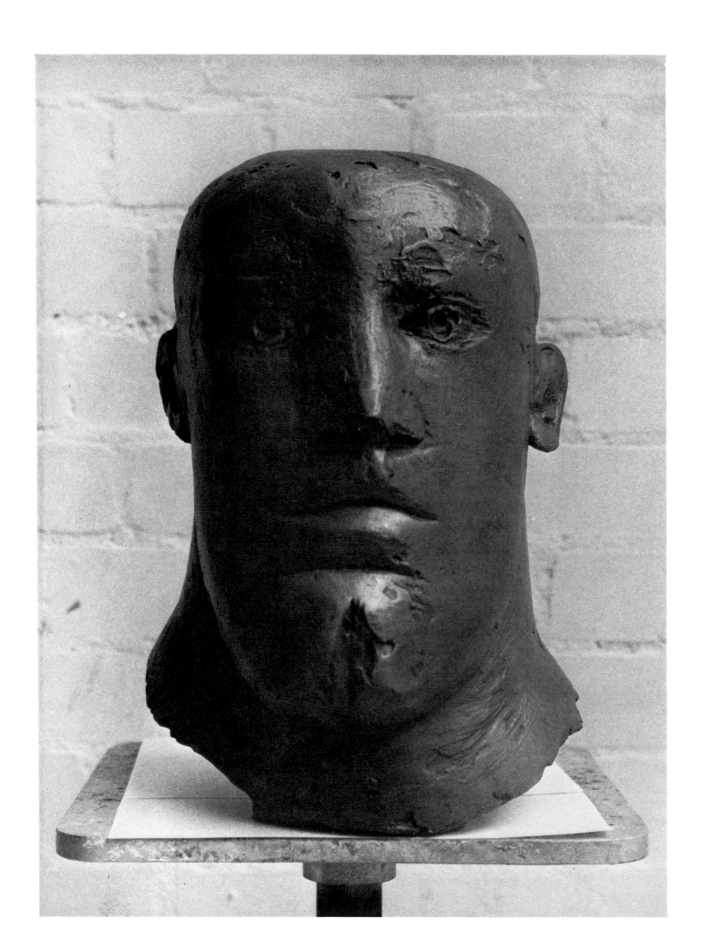

74 Two views of **New Bird I** bronze 21½/54·6 edition of 6 1965

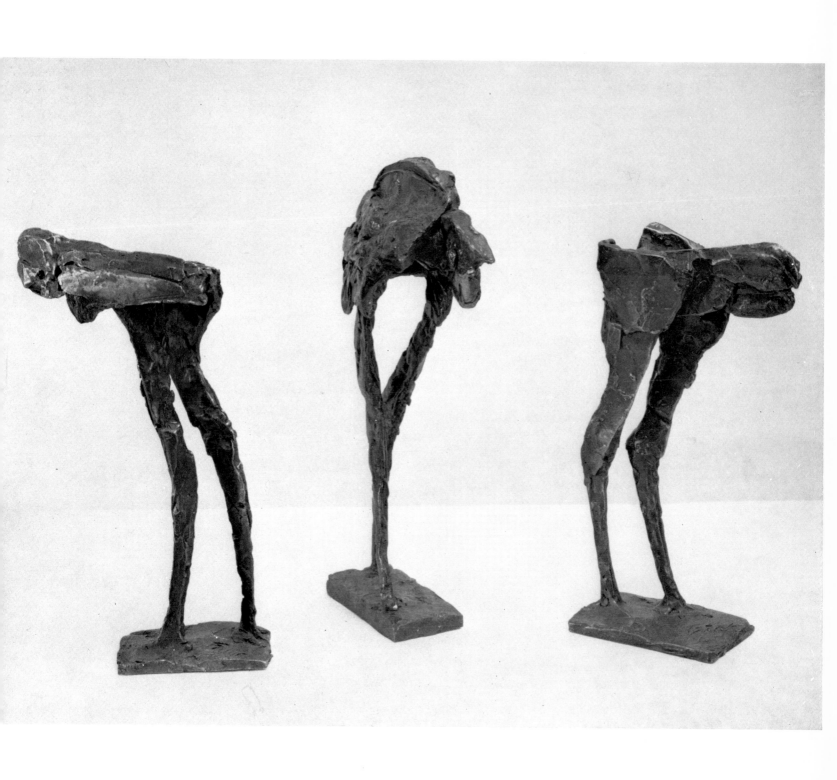

5 **Birds** bronze 8½/21·6, 10/25·4, 8½/21·6 all unique 1965

(left) **Homme Libellule I**
nze 16½/41·9
:ion of 6 1965

Homme Libellule II
nze 15/38·1
ion of 6 1965

Wild Boar bronze 6¼/15·9 edition of 7 1966

79 Homme Libellule III
bronze 18/45·7
edition of 7 1966

81 **Homme Libellule IV**
bronze 19/48·2
edition of 7 1966

82 (opposite) **Big Bird**
bronze c.20/50·8
edition of 6 1966–7

83 Bird
bronze 13⅞/35·2
edition of 6 1966

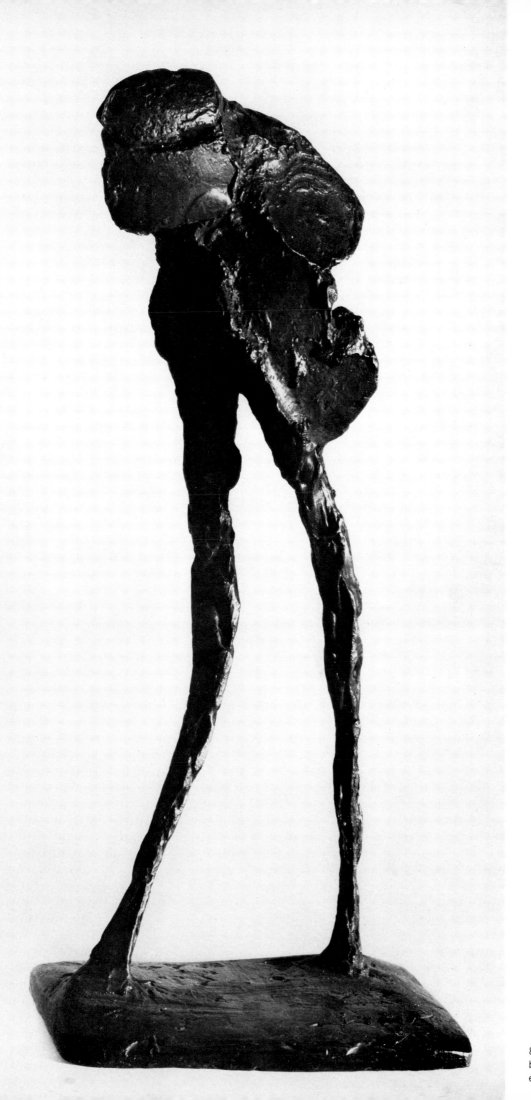

84 Bird
bronze 17/43·2
edition of 7 1966

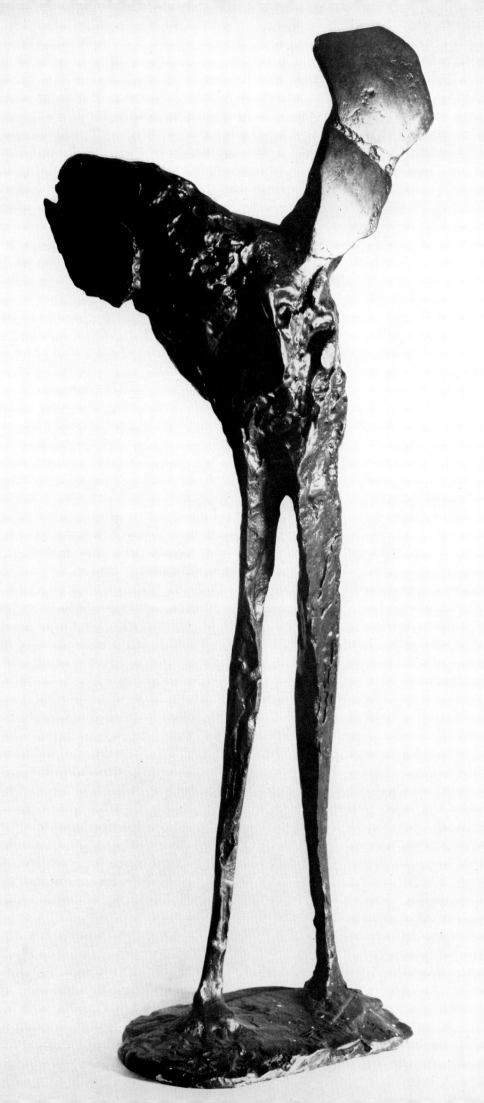

(left) **Bird with Wing** bronze 20/50·8 edition of 6 1966

(above) **Flying Figure** bronze L13/33 edition of 7 1966

87 **Wild Boar** bronze 6¼/15·9 edition of 7 1967
88 (opposite) **Wild Boar** bronze c.30/76·2 edition of 4 1967

Bronze Plaque bronze 8¾/22·2 edition of 8 1967

the following four pages:
Mirage Bird aluminium 84/213·4 edition of 3 1967
Mirage II bronze c.36/91·4 edition of 5 1967
Mirage I bronze 35¾/90·8 edition of 5 1967
Mirage bronze 33/83·8 edition of 6 1967

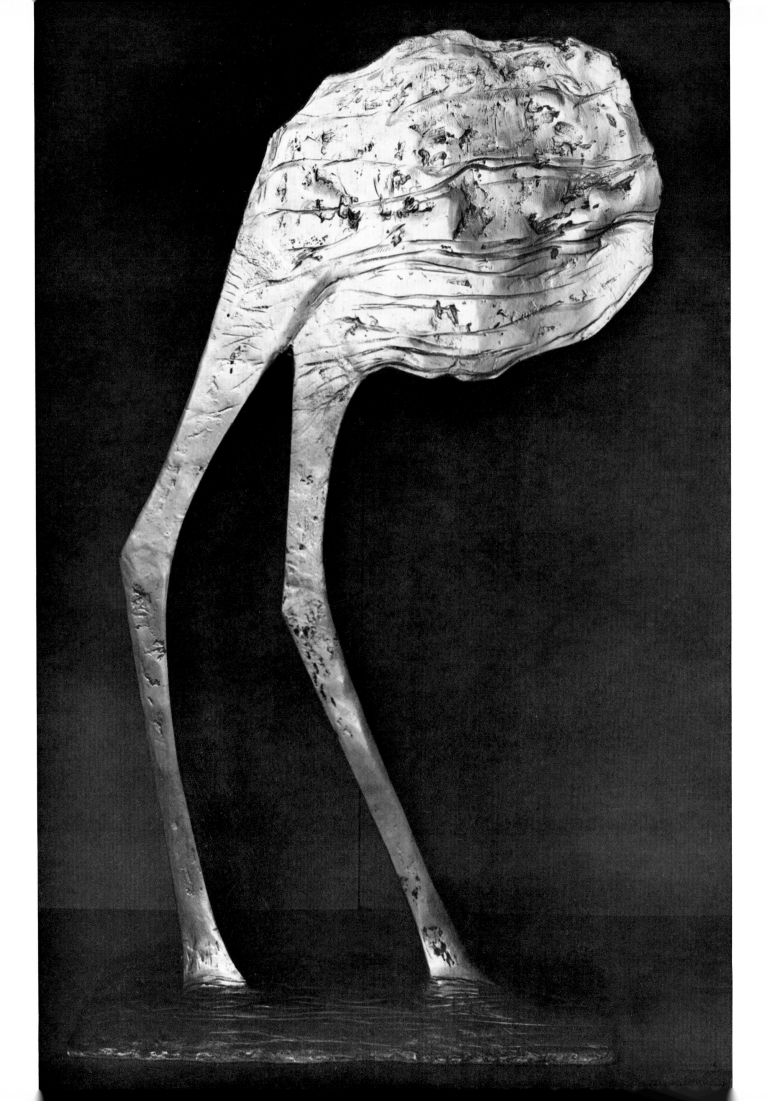

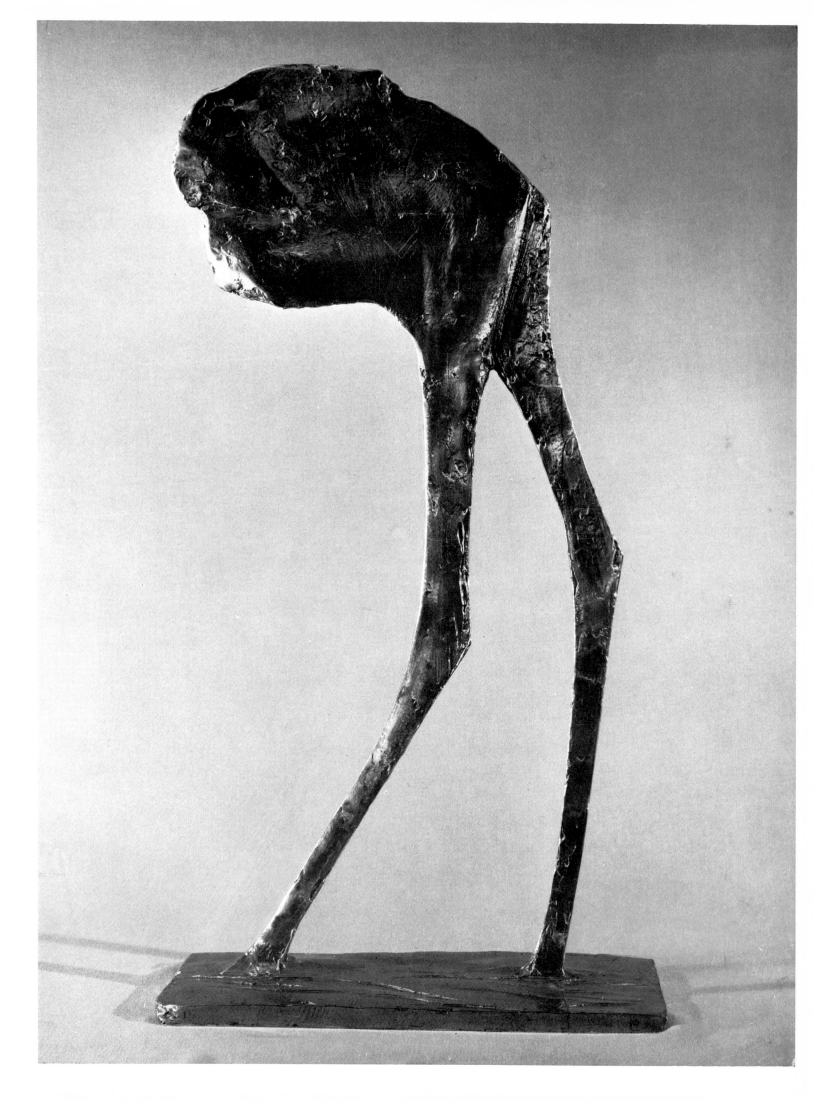

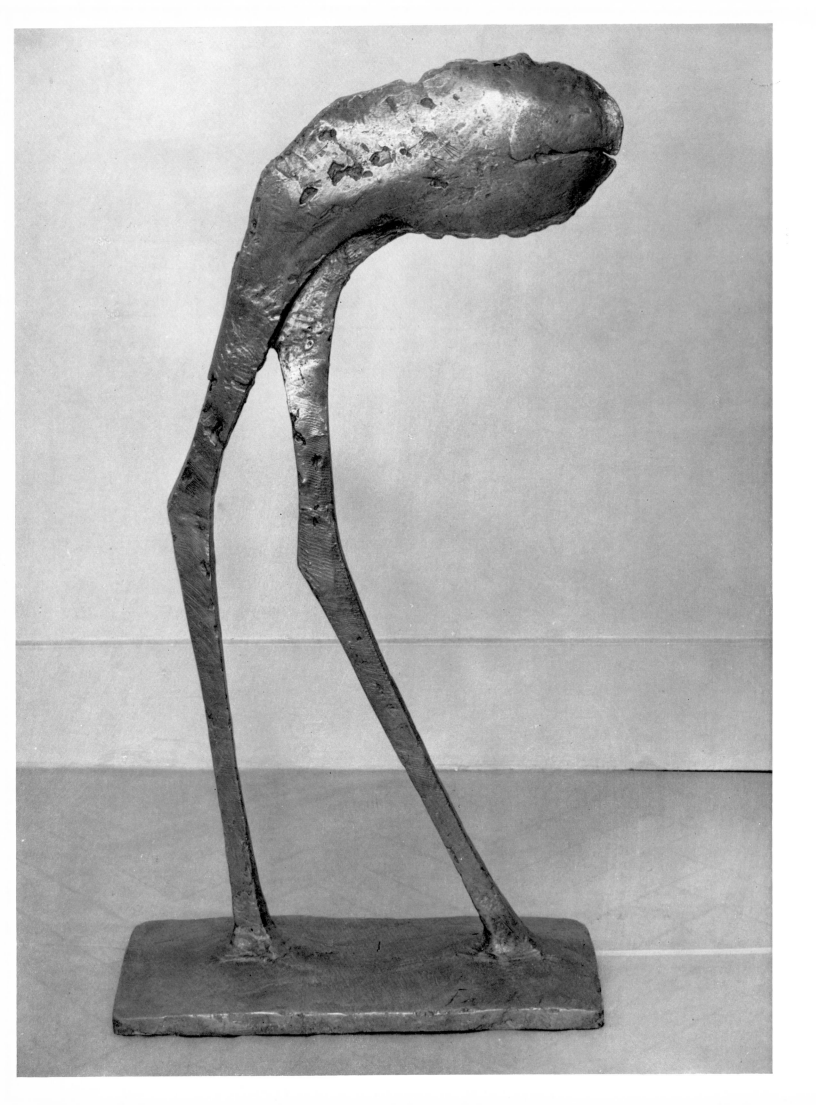

94 **Goggle Head (teeth)** bronze 20/50·8 edition of 6 1967
95 (opposite) another view of 94
96 (overleaf, left) **Head with Goggles** bronze 20/50·8 edition of 6 1967
97 (overleaf, right) **Head** bronze 21¾/55·2 edition of 6 1967

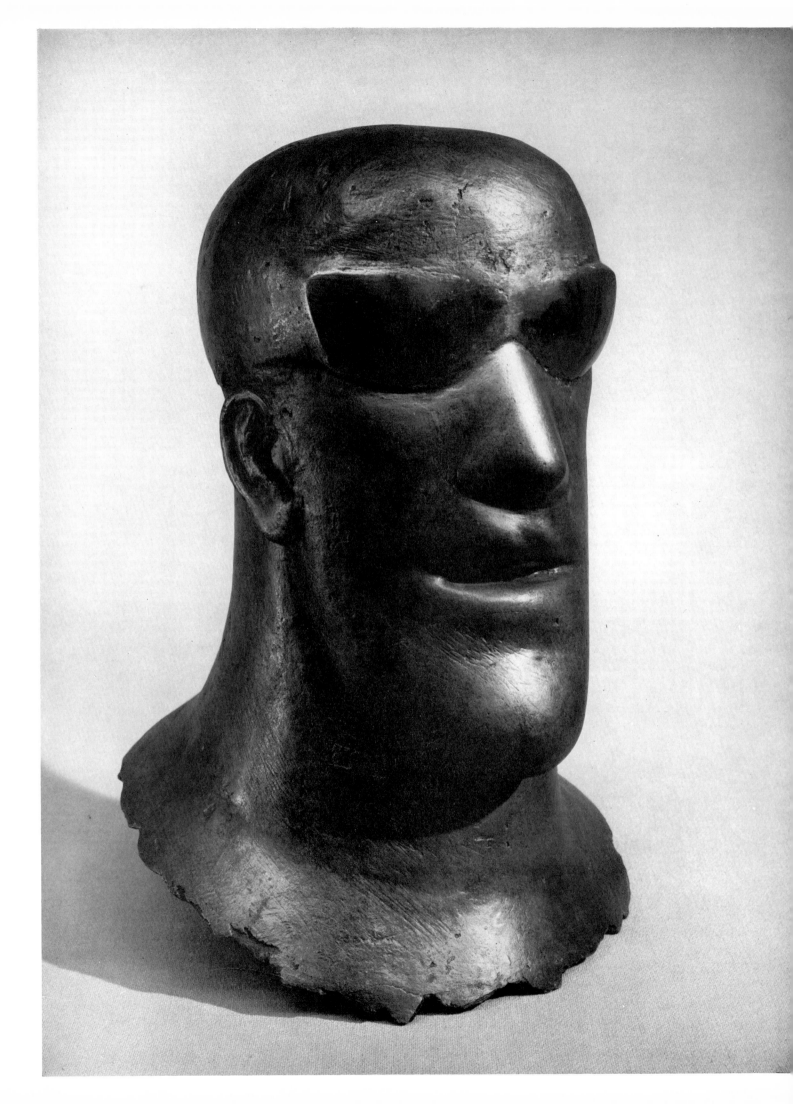

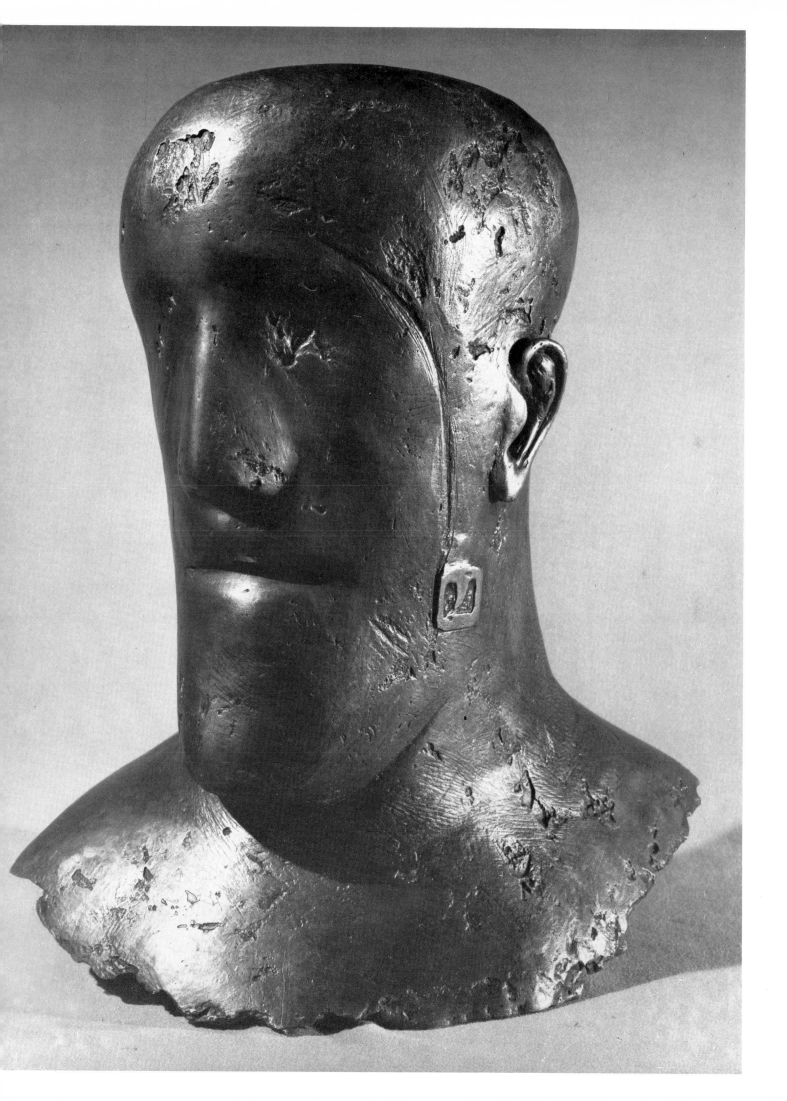

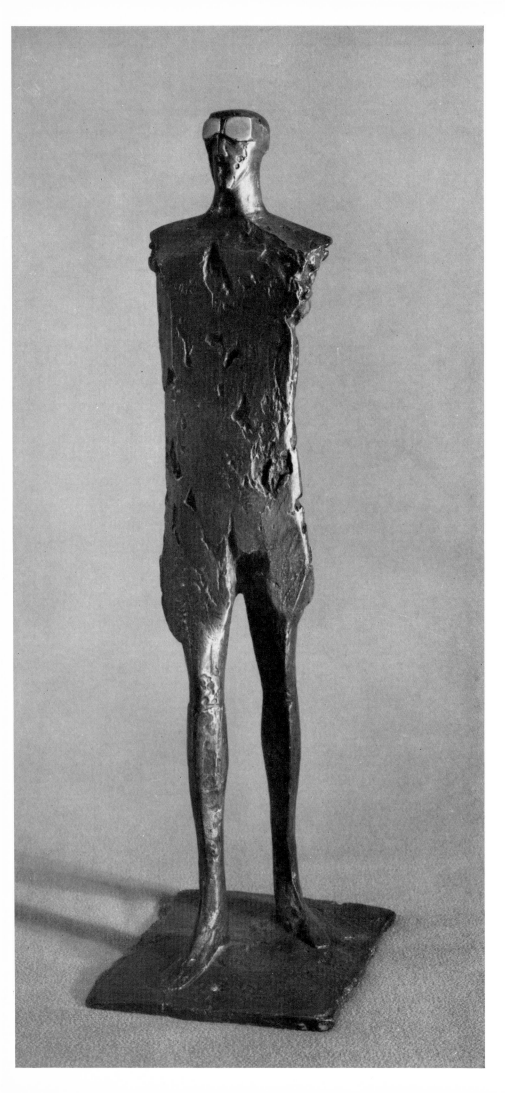

98 **Man with Goggles**
bronze 19½/49·5
edition of 7 1968
99 (opposite) **Small Walking Goggle Man**
bronze 18/45·7
edition of 7 1968

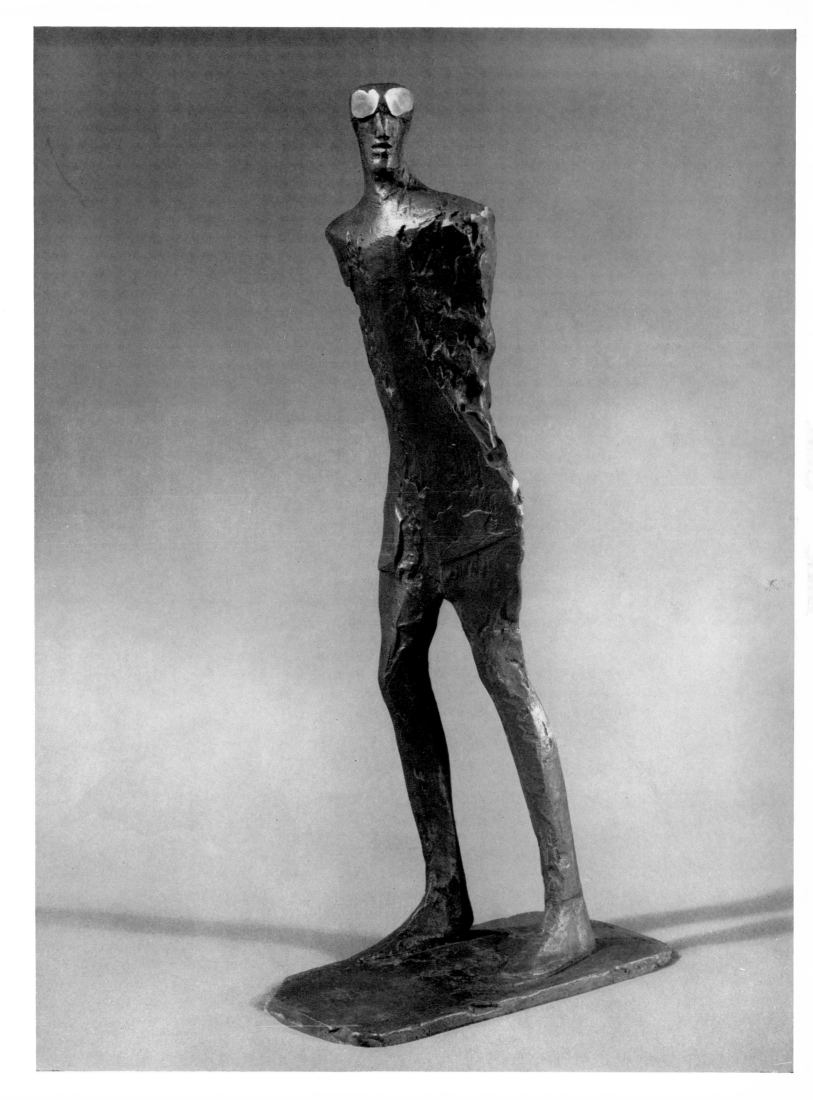

100 **Small Walking Goggle Man**
bronze 18/45·7
edition of 7 1968

101 (opposite) **Maquette for Crucifix, Liverpoo**
bronze 11½/29·2
unique 1968

Boar bronze 7/17·8 edition of 7 1969

103 **Boar** bronze 44/111·8 edition of 3 1969

105 (left) **Horse and Rider** plaster for bronze 90½/229·8 edition of 3 1969
106 (below) another view of 105

109 (opposite) **Mirage I** aluminium 108/274·3 unique 1969
110 (overleaf, left) **Head with Goggles (teeth)** bronze 25½/64·7 edition of 6 1969
111 (overleaf, right) **Head with Goggles (no teeth)** bronze 25½/64·7 edition of 6 1969

14

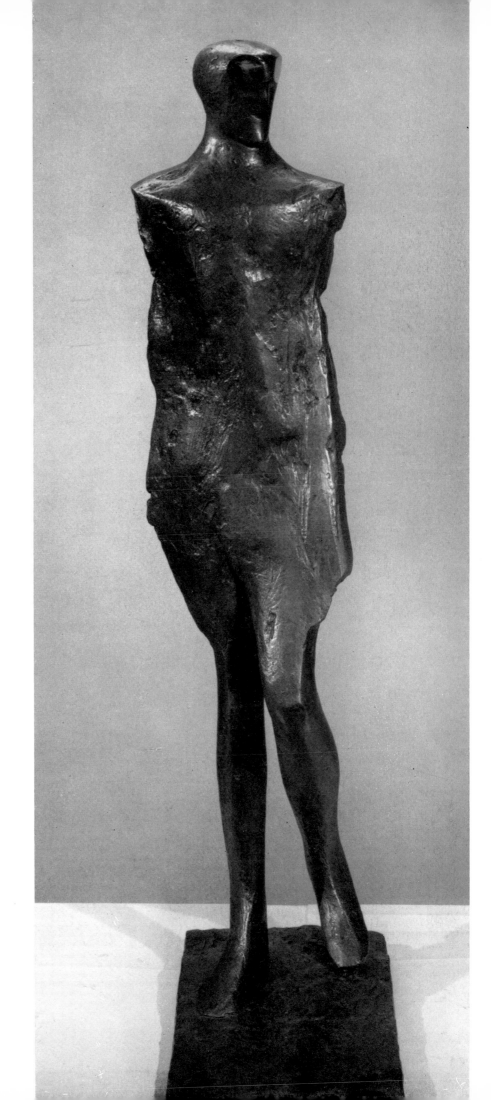

2 **Man with Goggles**
onze 44/111·7
ition of 6 1969

113 **Shooting Man** bronze 21/53·3 edition of 7 1970

Man on a Horse bronze 19¾/50·2 edition of 7 1970

115 **Small Boar** plaster for bronze 4½/11·4 1971

another view of 115

117 **Lying Down Horse** bronze 13/33 edition of 6 1971

Larger Rolling Over Horse bronze 15/38·1 editions of 6 1972

Sleeping Horse bronze life size edition of 4 1972

Lithographs

120 **Owl** 30½×23/77·5×58·4 edition of 25 1967

Wild Dog 31¼ × 23/79·4 × 58·4 edition of 25 1967

122 **Horse** 30½×23¼/77·5×59·1 edition of 25 1967

3 **Hare** 23¼×30½/59·1×77·5 edition of 70 1967

124 **Goat** 30½×23½/77·5×59·7 edition of 25 1967

Lioness 30½ × 23½ / 77·5 × 59·7 edition of 25 1967

126 **Boar** 21¼ × 25¾/54 × 65·4 edition of 70 1970

7 Bear 21¼×25¾/54×65·4 edition of 70 1970

128 **Man and Horse I** 23½×31½/59·7×80 edition of 70 1971

Man and Horse II 23½×31½/59·7×80 edition of 70 1971

130 **Man and Horse IV** 23½ × 31½/59·7 × 80 edition of 70 1971

1 **Man and Horse V** 23½×31½/59·7×80 edition of 70 1971

32 **Man and Horse VI** 23½×31½/59·7×80 edition of 70 1971

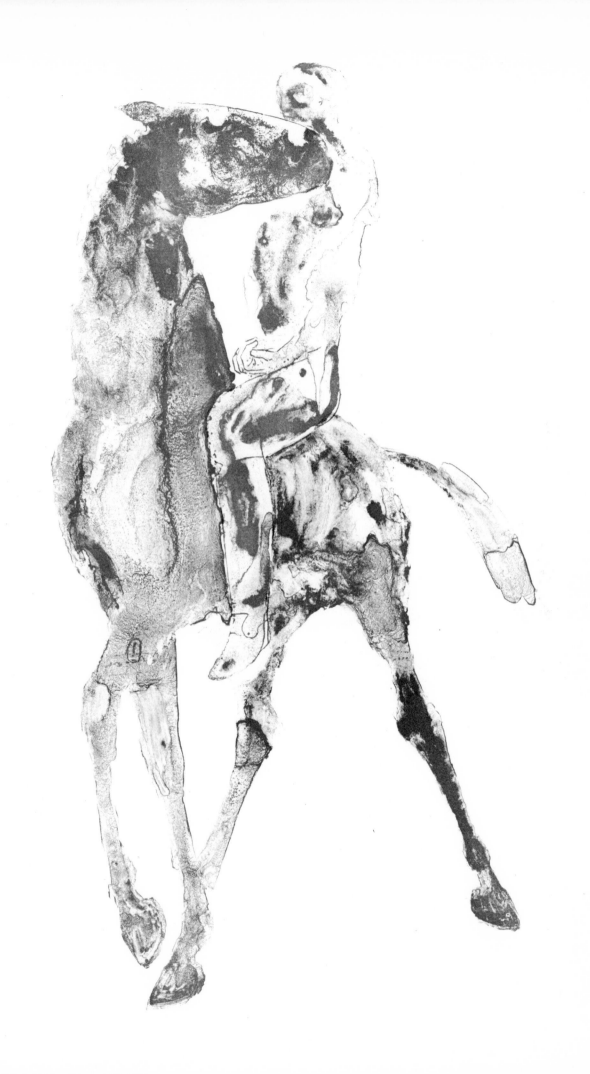

Horse and Rider IV 23×30½/58·4×77·5 edition of 70 1971

134 **Boar** 31¼ × 23¼/79·4 × 59·1 edition of 25 1967

Etchings : The Canterbury Tales

135 **The Franklin's Tale** 31½×22¾/80×57·8 edition ot 50 1972

136 **The Summoner's Tale** 31½×22¾/80×57·8 edition of 50 1972

137 **The Miller's Tale I** 31½×22¾/80×57·8 edition of 50 1972

138 **The Miller's Tale II** 31½×22¾/80×57·8 edition of 50 1972

139 **The Clerk's Tale** 31½×22¾/80×57·8 edition of 50 1972

140 **The Prologue** 31½ × 22¾/80 × 57·8 edition of 50 1972

141 The Nun's Priest's Tale 31½ × 22¾/80 × 57·8 edition of 50 1972

142 **Sir Topaz** 31½×22¾/80×57·8 edition of 50 1972

143 **The Merchant's Tale** 31½×22¾/80×57·8 edition of 50 1972

144 **The Reeve's Tale** 31½×22¾/80×57·8 edition of 50 1972

145 **The Second Nun's Tale** 31½×22¾/80×57·8 edition of 50 1972

146 **The Knight's Tale** 31½×22¾/80×57·8 edition of 50 1972

147 The Pardoner's Tale 31½×22¾/80×57·8 edition of 50 1972